But Is It Art?

Junk Sculpture

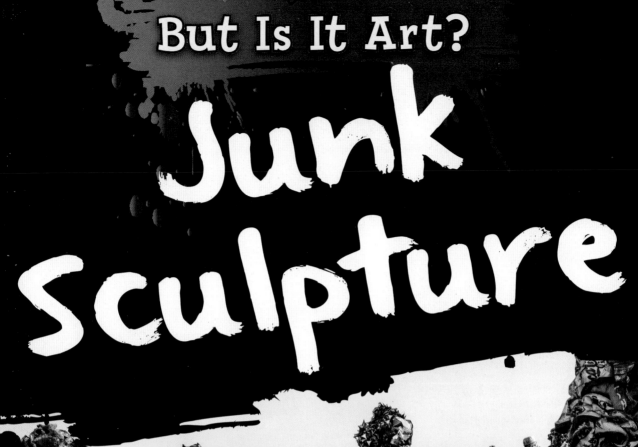

Alix Wood

Gareth Stevens
PUBLISHING

Please visit our website, **www.garethstevens.com**. For a free color catalog of all our high-quality books, call toll free 1-800-542-2595 or fax 1-877-542-2596

Library of Congress Cataloging-in-Publication Data

Wood, Alix.
 Junk sculpture / Alix Wood.
    pages cm. — (But is it art?)
 Includes bibliographical references and index.
 ISBN 978-1-4824-2287-0 (pbk.)
 ISBN 978-1-4824-2288-7 (6 pack)
 ISBN 978-1-4824-2285-6 (library binding)
 1. Junk sculpture—Juvenile literature. I. Title.
 NB198.5.J84W66 2015
 731'.2—dc23

                    2014033434

First Edition

Published in 2015 by
Gareth Stevens Publishing
111 East 14th Street, Suite 349
New York, NY 10003

© Alix Wood Books

Produced for Gareth Stevens by Alix Wood Books
Designed by Alix Wood
Editor: Eloise Macgregor

Photo credits:
Cover, 9, 12, 14, 20 top, 23, 32 © Shutterstock; 1, 6 © maratr/Shutterstock; 4 © Mcarse; 5, 29 © Aija Lehtonen/Shutterstock; 7 © Harry Hu/Shutterstock; 10 © Alfred Stieglitz; 11 top © Mark III Photonics/Shutterstock; 11 bottom © Featureflash/Shutterstock; 13 © Corbis; 15 top © Massimiliano Lamagna/Shutterstock; 15 bottom © Edwin Verin/Shutterstock; 16 © Dominic Alves; 17, 29 © The Zetetic; 18 © Evan Bench; 19 top © Watchtheworld/Shutterstock; 19 bottom © Gilsanz Murray Steficek; 20 bottom © Thelmadatter; 21 top © Museo de Arte Popular; 21 bottom © Nick Georgiou/My Human Computer; 22 © Blackinkwash; 24, 25, 28 © Robert Bradford; 26 © Andrew Whitehead; 27 © junrong/Shutterstock

Printed in the United States of America

CPSIA compliance information: Batch # CW15GS: For further information contact Gareth Stevens, New York, New York at 1-800-542-2595.

Contents

What Is Junk Sculpture? 4

Why Use Junk? 6

The *WEEE Man* 8

Ready-Made Sculpture 10

David Mach 12

Cadillac Ranch 14

Choosing the Materials 16

Tin Can Art 18

Paper Sculpture 20

Scarecrows 22

Toy Sculptures 24

Scrapyard Art 26

Is Junk Sculpture Art? 28

Glossary 30

For More Information 31

Index 32

What Is Junk Sculpture?

Junk sculpture is three-dimensional art made from things that people have thrown away. Art can be made out of anything! Some artists use junk as a way of **recycling** objects, instead of just chucking them in the trash. Using things that would otherwise be filling up **landfill** is good for the planet too.

Junk sculpture can be made out of all kinds of different materials. Next time you reach for the trash can, take a look at the thing you are throwing out. Could you turn it into something creative? Looking at junk sculpture helps you see trash in a whole new way!

Part of the fun of junk sculpture is working out what all the bits and pieces are. Can you see what this bird has been made out of?

Arty Fact

Junk sculpture is a new art form. Perhaps people would not have accepted junk sculpture as art before now. Modern living also creates more junk that we need to find uses for!

This pile of trash dumped outside a shopping center in Helsinki, Finland was created by **environmental** artist Kaisa Salmi. It looks like a mess! However the trash carries an important message. Salmi wanted to show people how much plastic was thrown away instead of being recycled.

Kaisa Salmi's piles of plastic waste. Can this be called a sculpture?

sculpture: a work created by carving or cutting hard substances, modeling plastic substances, or casting melted metals into works of art.

WHAT DO YOU THINK?

What's the difference between a pile of trash, and a pile of trash created by an artist? Is it art because the artist has thought about how they place the items? Or where they place them? Or why? Can a pile of trash mean something?

Different people have different ideas about what they think art is. Which of these do you agree with?

Art is:

- anything that an artist calls art
- something that is created with imagination and skill. It must be either beautiful, or express important ideas or feelings
- a mixture of "form" (the way something is created) and "content" (the "what" that has been created)

why Use Junk?

Sculptors get their **inspiration** from trash in different ways. Some simply see it as a great material to use. Others use it to get across an important message, such as encouraging recycling, or reducing waste. Other sculptors like the fact that junk is free!

German sculptor HA Schult makes sculptures out of trash because he believes we live in a time of garbage. He has created 1,000 human figures made from trash. He first exhibited them in Germany. People liked the figures, and he decided to take them on tour! Schult's sculpture *Trash People* has been displayed in the center of Paris, in Moscow's Red Square, at the Great Wall of China, and even in the desert next to the Pyramids of Giza, Egypt!

Trash People on tour in Tel Aviv, Israel

Some artists even use trash not just as a material but as a subject. They make sculptures OF trash, not OUT OF trash!

One night in 1976 Schult secretly filled St. Mark's Square in Venice, Italy with old newspapers. Schult wanted people to start thinking about trash and our society. Many local people were simply annoyed at the mess, however. In 2013 Schult created a heart out of garbage collected by schoolchildren, to show the children how much they are throwing away every day.

WHAT DO YOU THINK?

Does it matter why an artist uses junk? Is a sculpture more likely to be art if the sculptor had a message to get across? Or is it more likely to be art if he or she just thought the junk material made a great sculpture?

A catwalk model at a trashion show

Arty Fact

"Trashion" is the art of making fashion out of trash. The designers want to encourage people to make the best use of the planet's **resources**. Sometimes pieces are exhibited in galleries after trashion events.

The WEEE Man

Some junk sculptures are created to teach us something about how much we waste. *WEEE Man* was made out of discarded electrical items. "WEEE" stands for "waste, electrical, and electronic equipment." That means pretty much anything with a plug or battery!

WEEE Man was designed by London–based designer Paul Bonomini. It is a huge robot-like man made of scrap electrical and electronic equipment. It weighs 3.3 tons and stands 23 feet (7 m) tall! The sculpture is made out of the average amount of electrical and electronic goods each of us throws away over a lifetime.

WHAT DO YOU THINK?

WEEE Man has been designed to make us think about waste and recycling. Is a sculpture created to give an environmental message actually art, or is it something else?

Electronic waste is certainly a problem that we need to solve.

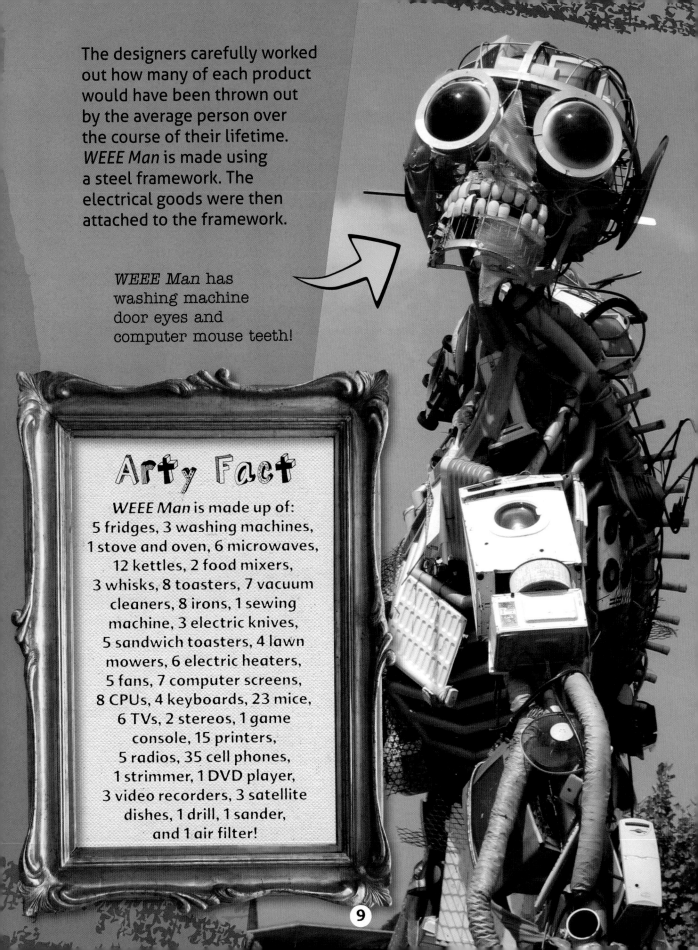

The designers carefully worked out how many of each product would have been thrown out by the average person over the course of their lifetime. *WEEE Man* is made using a steel framework. The electrical goods were then attached to the framework.

WEEE Man has washing machine door eyes and computer mouse teeth!

Arty Fact

WEEE Man is made up of: 5 fridges, 3 washing machines, 1 stove and oven, 6 microwaves, 12 kettles, 2 food mixers, 3 whisks, 8 toasters, 7 vacuum cleaners, 8 irons, 1 sewing machine, 3 electric knives, 5 sandwich toasters, 4 lawn mowers, 6 electric heaters, 5 fans, 7 computer screens, 8 CPUs, 4 keyboards, 23 mice, 6 TVs, 2 stereos, 1 game console, 15 printers, 5 radios, 35 cell phones, 1 strimmer, 1 DVD player, 3 video recorders, 3 satellite dishes, 1 drill, 1 sander, and 1 air filter!

Ready-Made Sculpture

Ready-made sculpture is when an artist selects an everyday object and displays it as art. One of the first ready-made artists was the Frenchman, Marcel Duchamp. His most famous work was a standard shop-bought urinal placed on its side on a pedestal! He called the sculpture *Fountain*.

Duchamp wanted to exhibit *Fountain* at the Society of Independent Artists exhibition in 1917. Usually all the pieces that were **submitted** were displayed in the exhibition. However, in this case, the show committee decided that his sculpture was not art. They would not allow it in the show. Duchamp resigned from the board of the Independent Artists in protest!

Marcel Duchamp's *Fountain*. The work was selected by art historians and well-known artists in 2004 as the most influential artwork of the 20th century!

WHAT DO YOU THINK?

If an artist hasn't altered a commonplace object in any way, but simply places it in an art gallery, can that be art? Has the artist changed our view of it? Have they recognized some beauty that we hadn't noticed, perhaps?

Several young British artists experiment with ready-made sculpture. Damien Hirst often uses animal carcasses as art. Tracey Emin once famously exhibited her own messy bed as an artwork at the Tate Gallery in London.

Tracey Emin

British artist Damien Hirst with one of his animals, preserved in **formaldehyde.** Hirst sometimes creates sculptures out of dead animals. This lamb is exactly as it was when it died. Hirst just preserved it.

Arty Fact

In May 2014 Tracey Emin's unmade bed was sold at auction for around $3.8 million dollars! That must mean someone thinks it's art!

David Mach

David Mach is a Scottish sculptor who works using old coat hangers, match heads, and magazines, amongst other things! One of his first sculptures was a Polaris submarine made out of thousands of car tires. The sculpture was meant as a protest against **nuclear arms**. Many journalists did not like the sculpture and wrote that it was not art, it was just a pile of tires.

Mach's *Out of Order* is a sculpture using 12 British telephone booths falling like dominoes.

WHAT DO YOU THINK?

Isn't any sculpture just a pile of marble or a lump of brass if you think about it? Mach's *Polaris* may have been made out of junk, but that doesn't mean the end result is junk. Should a sculpture be judged by the material it is made out of?

David Mach also likes to create a performance with his sculpture. He likes to set some of them on fire! Mach sometimes creates sculptures using matches. When he sets them alight, he doesn't see it as destroying a sculpture. He is creating a new one!

David Mach's coat hanger sculpture *Spaceman* is a tribute to Neil Armstrong's first moon landing.

Arty Fact

Mach first bends the coat hangers around a plastic molded base. Then he welds the hangers together. He removes the mold and nickel-plates the sculptures to finish.

Cadillac Ranch

If you half-bury ten Cadillacs in the ground, is that art? *Cadillac Ranch* in Amarillo, Texas is a sculpture created by an artist's group called Ant Farm. The piece uses ten different models of Cadillac cars from between 1949 and 1963.

Cadillac Ranch was created in 1974 by Chip Lord, Hudson Marquez, and Doug Michels. These large Cadillacs were not popular then. Most of them were bought cheaply from junkyards. They would have been crushed years ago if they hadn't been turned into a sculpture!

Cadillac Ranch is always changing due to the work of graffiti artists. Can you see the discarded spray cans on the ground?

Arty Fact

The cars are buried nose-first in the ground. They are positioned at the same angle as the sides of the Great Pyramid of Giza in Egypt!

Graffiti is encouraged at the site. The cars are popular with graffiti artists. Now and then the cars are all painted in one color, sometimes to celebrate a birthday. They were once all painted black when Ant Farm member Doug Michels died. Sometimes the graffiti is painted over just to provide a fresh canvas for graffiti artists.

The cadillacs after a fresh coat of yellow paint.

The sculptures stand along the well-known road, Route 66. The road was the main highway heading west across the US from Chicago to California.

WHAT DO YOU THINK?

When does a car become art? Is it a sculpture itself even before you bury it in the ground? Can something be considered a sculpture if it is mass produced? Some cars certainly are beautiful!

The ten different cadillac models show how car styles changed over the years, particularly their tail fins.

Choosing the Materials

Sometimes the choice of materials that an artist uses is as important as the sculpture itself. When an artist chooses a particular type of junk, that choice may give the sculpture added importance. The sculptor may be trying to make us think, not just about waste, but about other problems in our world.

Nick Sayers homeless shelter made from old realtor's signs.

Designer Nick Sayers made this shelter out of old house "for sale" signs. He could have made the sculpture out of any material. His choice of discarded "for sale" boards makes people who view the sculpture think about property and homelessness. While many people are making money from selling houses, there are people who simply need somewhere to shelter.

WHAT DO YOU THINK?

Nick Sayers uses his work to highlight waste and "visual clutter" in our world. Visual clutter means things like too many road signs or advertising. Do you think there are too many signs and advertisements in your neighborhood?

Arty Fact

Brazilian artist Tonico Lemos Auad makes sculptures using carpet fluff! He likes to work with materials that are not easily noticeable, or that vanish under our eyes. He fills an area with carpet dust and fluff. He then creates tiny animals by pulling the fluff with his fingers!

Why an artist decides to use a material is a personal choice. The artist may just be inspired by the look of the object. Or want to recycle it rather than waste it. The artist may just like how the sun shines through it! Junk sculpture inspires us to look at everyday objects in a new way.

Do you think this sculpture looks like art? It's actually just a pile of junk that was found when clearing out a local creek. Does that matter? If we think a pile of junk looks great, does it matter that it wasn't created by an artist?

Tin Can Art

Recycling drink cans really helps our environment by creating less waste. Making a sculpture out of the cans is a really cool way to recycle them! Can sculptures can be beautiful and brighten up a city park, such as the dragon sculpture below. Some sculptures make us think, such as the **tsunami** memorial opposite. Sculptures can even encourage generosity, by donating the food in the tins to charity.

This soda can dragon is made of aluminum cans. It is in the Zoological Park in Paris, France. The smoke that comes from the dragon's mouth is made of shredded plastic bags.

The can dragon sculpture shimmers in the sunlight.

Japanese sculptor Sayaka Ganz believes the best way that artists can help reduce waste is to show people how beautiful these waste materials can be. If we value them, we will waste less.

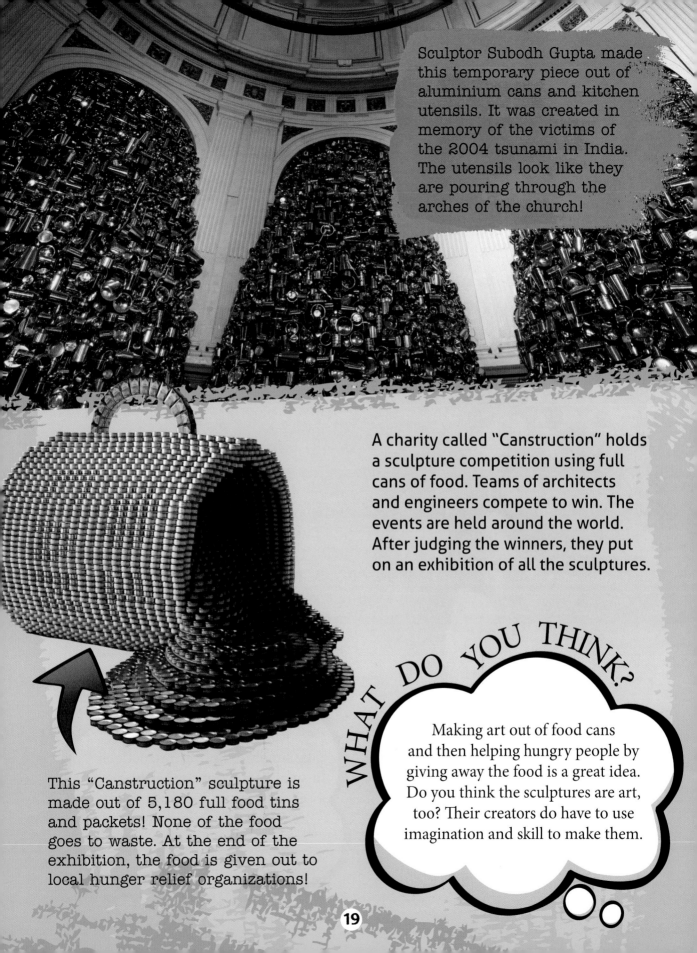

Sculptor Subodh Gupta made this temporary piece out of aluminium cans and kitchen utensils. It was created in memory of the victims of the 2004 tsunami in India. The utensils look like they are pouring through the arches of the church!

A charity called "Canstruction" holds a sculpture competition using full cans of food. Teams of architects and engineers compete to win. The events are held around the world. After judging the winners, they put on an exhibition of all the sculptures.

This "Canstruction" sculpture is made out of 5,180 full food tins and packets! None of the food goes to waste. At the end of the exhibition, the food is given out to local hunger relief organizations!

WHAT DO YOU THINK?

Making art out of food cans and then helping hungry people by giving away the food is a great idea. Do you think the sculptures are art, too? Their creators do have to use imagination and skill to make them.

19

Paper Sculpture

Paper is a great material to make sculpture out of. It's cheap and can be folded, scrunched up, stuck with paste, or cut into shapes.

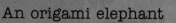

An origami elephant

Some countries make traditional paper sculptures. The Japanese fold paper to make origami sculptures. They often fold the paper into animals or fish shapes. Traditional Mexican piñatas are popular at birthday parties. The hollow, paper piñata is filled with sweets and hung on a piece of string above everyone's heads. People are blindfolded and take turns hitting the piñata with a stick.

This crazy coral reef piñata won a piñata contest at a Mexico City art museum.

WHAT DO YOU THINK?

Paper folding can be done by simply following instructions in an origami book. Is that as artistic as thinking up your own paper folding? Or creating your own colorful piñata?

Are you feeling inspired? Try making a junk sculpture yourself. You can make anything that your imagination can think of. Perhaps make a frame from an old coat hanger or from chicken wire. Cover the frame with strips of old newspaper stuck on with flour and water paste. Once the sculpture has dried you can paint it, or decorate it by sticking small bits of junk onto the surface. You might need an adult to help you bend the wire.

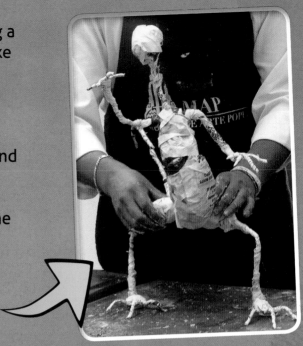

A wire frame covered with newspaper and glue makes a great junk sculpture.

Henry Moore : A sculptor is a person who is interested in the shape of things, a poet in words, a musician by sounds.

A paper sculpture made from old newspapers by Nick Georgiou.

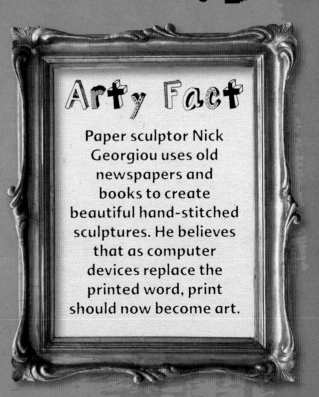

Arty Fact

Paper sculptor Nick Georgiou uses old newspapers and books to create beautiful hand-stitched sculptures. He believes that as computer devices replace the printed word, print should now become art.

Scarecrows

Scarecrows have been used for thousands of years by farmers to help scare the birds away from crops in the fields. They are usually made using two sticks to make a cross shape, with a head stuck on the top. People then put clothes on the figures and stick them in the ground to scare the birds. Some people have turned scarecrow-making into art.

Many villages around the world hold scarecrow festivals. People compete to make the best scarecrow, and display them around the village for people to see, and for a winner to be awarded. Scarecrows are quite easy to make. Clear out some old clothes and try yourself!

WHAT DO YOU THINK?

If something has been created for a purpose, can it still be art? When scarecrows were first invented they were not thought of as art. If a scarecrow is an exhibit at a festival it might be art, but what about if it is in a field scaring crows?

At village scarecrow festivals, local people make scarecrows, like this one, and display them outside their home.

This field of scarecrows in Finland was created by the artist Reijo Kela. There are around a thousand scarecrows in the field! The sculpture is called *Silent People*. A local youth group looks after them, changing their outfits twice a year! The sculptures appear magical and mysterious. At different times of day they can look either fun and happy, or very sinister and scary.

Arty Fact

2500 years ago Greek farmers carved wooden scarecrows to look like a boy named Priapus. When Priapus played in his vineyards the birds stayed away from the grapes. Other farmers made statues that looked like Priapus, so they would get a good harvest, too!

Kela created another *Silent People* in a field in Kent, England. They were put up overnight, and surprised local people when they woke up the following morning. Some of the scarecrows were vandalized, with several figures destroyed. In reply, some scarecrows were given black armbands as a tribute to their lost comrades!

Toy Sculptures

Looking in his children's toybox one day, sculptor Robert Bradford discovered a new material. He liked the colors and shapes that the toys made when they were placed together. He started making huge sculptures out of discarded toys.

One of the fun things about Bradford's sculptures is that they are a history of toy fashion as well as being amazing works of art. You can pretty much tell the year each sculpture was made by the toys that are used!

Can you recognize any toys you played with in this rabbit?

Arty Fact

Bradford wasn't sure how to join the plastic toys together. He thought using screws would split the plastic. After trying other methods, he found that usually the plastic didn't crack when he screwed them together, after all.

Most trash doesn't give you the strong memories that old toys can bring back. Bradford's sculptures are full of childhood memories. What memories do you have when you look at his sculptures?

Most people like looking at the toy sculptures. They get enjoyment from the sculpture as a whole, and from looking at all the tiny pieces that make up the figure. The memories they bring are different for everyone, so the sculpture is unique to each person who looks at it!

This piece is called *Toy Soldier*.

25

Scrapyard Art

Many junk sculptors take inspiration from the scrapyard. Working with large pieces of metal may need special skills, such as **welding**, but the results are really worth it!

When you look at a pile of old rusting tools, it's hard to imagine that they can create something as beautiful as the horse and jockey sculpture below. Andrew Whitehead is an Australian sculptor who works using scrap metal. He collects old rusty tools from the farms around his home in New South Wales to create his sculptures.

Whitehead's horse and jockey took about six months to complete. The horse alone weighs around half a ton! Whitehead made the piece in sections that can be carried separately and then put together.

Scrapyards usually charge for their metal. Scrap metal can be quite valuable. One scrapyard in Tennessee arranged for twelve local sculptors to take away as much scrap as they could in one day as part of an arts project. The artists donated them a sculpture in return.

WHAT DO YOU THINK?

What do you think is the best use for old scrap metal? Should it be reused in a sculpture? Or is it better if it's recycled to manufacture something more useful, like a car?

This junk sculpture is displayed at the Kailuan National Mine Park in China. The band must be playing heavy metal!

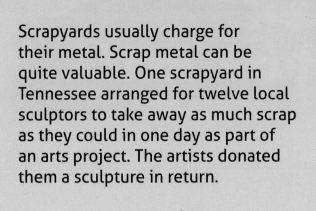

Is Junk Sculpture Art?

Have you made up your mind? Is junk sculpture art? To help you, have a look at some of these arguments "for" and "against."

Junk Sculpture IS Art

- If the artists call it art, it must be art

- The sculptures can be beautiful

- Junk sculptures can be skillfully put together

- Any sculpture can brighten the area where it is put

- The artists are expressing themselves

- Museums and galleries exhibit junk sculpture, so it must be art

- Some sculptures are giving an important political message

Junk Sculpture ISN'T Art

- Sculptures made from old junk don't look very nice

- A pile of junk can't be art

- Junk sculpture is too easy to make to be art

- Ready-made junk sculptures aren't art, because the artist hasn't changed them in any way

- Scarecrows can't be art, they are just for scaring crows

- Junk is not a proper art material like marble or stone is

Remember these two piles of trash? The one on the left was intended to be art. The one on the right is just a pile of trash. Which one looks most like art to you? Why?

Junk sculpture could be thought of as more skillful than most other types of sculpture. It is much easier to make a beautiful piece of marble or brass look appealing than a pile of old plastic bottles!

Arty Fact

There are many artists working at creating junk sculpture pieces. If so many artists think that what they are doing is art, they can't all be wrong. One man's junk is another man's treasure.

WHAT DO YOU THINK?

If you are not sure, that's OK. Perhaps some junk sculpture could be called art and some couldn't? Which artists or types of junk sculpture do you think could be called art?

Glossary

environmental
Concerned with the harmful effects of events that are altering the environment.

formaldehyde
A colorless gas that consists of carbon, hydrogen, and oxygen, has a sharp, irritating odor, and when dissolved in water is used to disinfect or to prevent decay.

inspiration
Someone or something that stimulates a higher activity or causes a particular thought or feeling.

landfill
A system of trash and garbage disposal in which the waste is buried between layers of earth.

nuclear arms
Weapons that involve a nuclear reaction.

recycling
Processing items such as glass, plastics, or cans in order to regain materials for human use.

resources
A usable stock or supply of something.

submitted
To have put forward a work of art for inclusion in an exhibition.

tsunami
A great sea wave, usually produced by an earthquake or volcanic eruption under the sea.

welding
Joining pieces of metal or plastic by heating and allowing the edges to flow together or by hammering or pressing together.

For More Information

Books

Carter, David, and James Diaz: *You Call That Art?!: Learn About Modern Sculpture and Make Your Own.* New York, NY: Abrams Books for Young Readers, 2014.

Hanson, Anders: *Cool Sculpture: The Art of Creativity for Kids!.* Edina, MN: Checkerboard Books, 2008.

Scheunemann, Pam: *Cool Metal Projects: Creative Ways to Upcycle Your Trash Into Treasure.* Edina, MN: Checkerboard Books, 2012.

Websites

Activity Village
http://www.activityvillage.co.uk/recycling-crafts
Fun junk modeling ideas for kids to create their own sculptures.

Tate Kids
http://kids.tate.org.uk/create/
Art activities such as soap carving and making things from junk.

Publisher's note to educators and parents:
Our editors have carefully reviewed these websites to ensure that they are suitable for students. Many websites change frequently, however, and we cannot guarantee that a site's future contents will continue to meet our high standards of quality and educational value. Be advised that students should be closely supervised whenever they access the Internet.

Index

A
Ant Farm 14, 15
Auad, Tonico Lemos 17

B
Bonomini, Paul 8
Bradford, Robert 24, 25

C
Cadillac Ranch 14, 15

D
Duchamp, Marcel 10

E
Emin, Tracey 11

F
Fountain 10

G
Ganz, Sayaka 18
Georgiou, Nick 21
Gupta, Subodh 19

H
Hirst, Damien 11

K
Kela, Reijo 23

M
Mach, David 12, 13
Moore, Henry 21

O
Out of Order 12

S
Salmi, Kaisa 5
Sayers, Nick 16
Schult, HA 6, 7
Silent People 23
Spaceman 13

T
Trash People 6
trashion 7

W
WEEE Man 8, 9
Whitehead, Andrew 26